Letter to the Americans

Letter to the Americans

Jean Cocteau

translated from the French
by Alex Wermer-Colan

A NEW DIRECTIONS PAPERBOOK ORIGINAL

Originally published in French as *Lettre aux Américains*

COMITÉ
Jean Cocteau   This edition is published with the kind authorization
*   of Comité Jean Cocteau

First published as New Directions Paperbook 1529 in 2022
Manufactured in the United States of America
Design by Erik Rieselbach

Library of Congress Cataloging-in-Publication Data
Names: Cocteau, Jean, 1889–1963, author. | Wermer-Colan, Alex, translator.
Title: Letter to the Americans / Jean Cocteau ; translated from the French
by Alex Wermer-Colan.
Other titles: Lettre aux Américains. English
Description: New York : New Directions Publishing Corporation, [2022] |
"A New Directions Paperbook original."
Identifiers: LCCN 2021054381 | ISBN 9780811231596 (paperback)
Subjects: LCSH: United States—Civilization. | National characteristics,
American. | New York (N.Y.)—Civilization.
Classification: LCC E169.1 .C613 2022 | DDC 973—dc23/eng/20211108
LC record available at https://lccn.loc.gov/2021054381

10 9 8 7 6 5 4 3 2 1

New Directions Books are published for James Laughlin
by New Directions Publishing Corporation
80 Eighth Avenue, New York 10011

Letter to the Americans

AMERICANS,

I'm writing you from the plane that's bringing me back to France. I spent twenty days in New York and I did so much and saw so many people that I can't tell if I visited your home for twenty days or twenty years. You'll tell me that one can't judge a country by a city, America by New York, and that my stay was too brief for me to dare permit myself. But in some cases the first look you cast over a face reveals more than prolonged study. Sometimes you stare so long at a person that you revise your first impression, only for the judgment you make on a second glance to trick you further. The third look and all the following allow you to tolerate a person and, thereby, to become a bad judge, since sound judgments can only be made from the outside. If you live with people, you come to feel a groggy confusion where the contours of personalities blend. Sometimes a city thinks it bears little resemblance to other cities, reflecting immense territories whose clocks don't correspond, where the night of some is the day of others, where some are awake while others sleep. I mean that some are preoccupied by the absurd magnificence of a dream while others act without dreaming. This provokes, without anyone suspecting, a circulation of waves that the soul registers but that the mind can't decipher. It's no less true that these waves spread out and give themselves to an obscure labor. It's also likely that New Yorkers' appetite for a world that wrests them from their own arises from this considerable tide of dreams, and that the perpetual cross-examination to which New Yorkers subject this dream represents their defensive weapon, the wall, the dam that prevents them from becoming completely engulfed.

For this attraction that enigmas exert and this horror of enigmas is the grand affair of the American spirit.

IN NEW YORK, everything is paradoxical. You need the new but want nothing to change. The provisional failure at the beginning of all great enterprises remains incomprehensible to you; instead you take it to be the irrevocable outcome. Success to you is compulsory—it's the tragedy of the movie industry, since all the muses know how to wait, must be painted and represented in the attitude of waiting, and grow younger in the long run instead of older. Even if painting, sculpture, music, and poetry can wait, only triumphing after the death of the person that they convey, a film can't wait, costs too much to wait, and must succeed monstrously on the very first shot.

I'll speak again about these things. For the moment, I release myself to the rhythm of the propellers and to this strange realm of memories that dwell within us. They move like underwater plants and, each time they touch each other, they disperse in different directions.

NEW YORK ISN'T a sitting city. It's not a reclining city. New York is a standing city, and not because of the skyscrapers where numbers (which devour New York) established their anthill. I speak of a standing city because, if she sat down, she would repose and reflect, and because, if she lay down, she would sleep and dream. Since she wants neither to reflect nor to dream, she stands divided between the two breasts of her mother, one flowing with alcohol and the other with milk. She wants to remain standing, to forget (what?), to forget herself, to wear herself out, to exhaust herself, to escape, by fatigue and the imperceptible swaying of drunks and of skyscrapers with immobile foundations and wobbling pinnacles, to escape, I say, the interrogation that you give to yourself, that you fear to give to yourself, and to which you subject others continually.

Humanity is occupied by a darkness, by monsters from profound zones. We can't descend the depths, but sometimes, through the intercessions of poets, this darkness dispatches ambassadors terrible enough. These ambassadors intrigue you. They attract and repulse you. You try to understand their language, and being incapable, you ask the poets to translate for you. Alas! the poets don't understand it any better and content themselves to act as the humble servants of these ambassadors, the mediums for these individualistic phantoms that haunt you, that disturb you, that you would love to unionize.

NEW YORK DETESTS *the secret*. She pries into those of others. She disavows her own, like the Ennui she exorcises with methodical optimism.

New York is open, a wide-open city. Her arms are open, her faces are open, her hearts are open, open streets, doors, windows. This creates a euphoria for the visitor, a current of air where ideas can't ripen and whirl instead like dead leaves.*

I repeat: You refuse to wait and to keep waiting. In New York, everyone arrives ahead of time to the meeting. Tradition revolts you, as does the new. Your ideal would be *an instantaneous tradition*. The new is immediately canonized. From this minute it ceases to exist. You classify it, you label it, and, since you don't permit artists to experiment, you demand that they repeat themselves and you replace them when they bore you. This is how you kill flies.

I saw, at the Museum of Modern Art, an unforgettable spectacle.** In a spotless nursery, fifty little girls paint on tables piled high with brushes, inks, tubes, and gouache. They paint while looking elsewhere

---

* No trees in New York. The trees have a suspicious air, as if dreaming.
** Thanks to Monroe Wheeler, this museum is an example of order and beauty. One finds between other marvels *The Sleeping Gypsy* by Rousseau and *Guernica* by Picasso, waiting to find its place in a new Spain.

and sticking out their tongues in the manner of performing animals that ring a bell, tongue lolling and eyes vague. Nannies survey these young creatures of abstract art, and give them a slap on the hand if, by accident, their paintings begin to represent something, teetering dangerously towards realism. The mothers (who stay by Picasso) aren't admitted. In the galleries, next to masterpieces by Rousseau, Matisse, Picasso, Braque, Bonnard, Vuillard, they hang the dirty laundry of our adolescence, our stains of ink and wine on old napkins from the Rotonde and the Dome. For New York is a tall giraffe, spotted with windows, loaded with relics.

How to explain to this youthful, note-taking crowd that audacity doesn't always appear garbed in the vestments of audacity, that what really matters is the spirit of revolt, and that we must now contradict ourselves and baffle the youth again with new audacities that they'll mistake for regressions?

I OBSERVE, ON my right, a woman dozing, her face caught in a beard of orchids. On her lap *Life Maga-zine* is spread open. It is, it seems to me, the publication that possesses one of the largest readerships in America. And I see again, with my eyes closed in turn, my recent journey and that Sunday night in New York. *Life Magazine* had pleaded to take a se-ries of eccentric photographs of me. When I told the journalists that neither my age, nor my position as a poet (that is to say, a laborer), gave me the right to let them take eccentric photographs of me, they replied that it was customary and that their readers were solely interested in such photographs. Since I was New York's guest, I yielded to their request and suggested a few fitting themes to appease them, to compromise myself only to the extent that I'm will-ing to be compromised.

We worked from three in the afternoon until seven. I dined with Jacques Maritain. We then re-sumed our work from eleven o'clock until five in the morning. There was a break around two. Sandwiches and ginger ale. It was then that the journalists and the photographer for *Life* said to me this surprising thing: "What could a man at the barber, in the midst of looking at *Life Magazine*, in the darkest depths of Massachusetts, make of these photographs? Don't you fear they'll unsettle him?" "But," I responded, "these extravagances don't come from me. They come from you." They fluctuated between anguished doubt and certainty that photographs of this type were the only valuable ones. Then they brought up the serious problem of captioning, asking me how one could explain the inexplicable. I suggested that the photographs they'd taken were really quite normal, that the camera had played a trick on them, that they would have to apologize to the public, that machines were clearly becoming hazardous to the image of humanity. Append, I told them, an advertisement for Rolleiflex. For example: *Rolleiflex thinks.*

This anecdote is a typical example of the American paradox. Ceaselessly, in your home, you find yourself nose-to-nose with audacity and the fear of audacity. It's gotten to the point that, in your theaters, passion needs to be pathological, curable or, otherwise, in the end, punished. Passion must present itself with an excuse. Passion must result from madness or alcohol. Imagination, in the movies, must be governed by dreams: if a man falls asleep at the beginning of the film and wakes up at the end, the director can indulge in anything and go anywhere.

If you're in need of excuses, are you therefore guilty? Do you recognize yourselves as guilty? When your censor, in submission to the strange psychosis of the *bed* as shameful furniture, representative of love and of dreams, your two obsessions, your two terrors, reproaches me for the scene between the son and the mother in my film *Les Parents Terribles*, aren't you ashamed, you, noble people, of an ignoble thought, don't you see what inhibition forces you to interpret kindness and innocence as evil?

You deify Van Gogh and I approve.

But isn't Van Gogh the perfect example of the artist who dies in misery? Which is exactly what New York despises most of all.

In this respect you imitate the rest of the globe, for if they hadn't burned Joan of Arc, she wouldn't be a heroine and we wouldn't be able to make films about her.*

* I point out to you in passing that the world champion Al Brown, the genius of boxing, currently mopes about in Harlem, alone, unknown, without a dime.

I WRITE "YOU," but it's not you, the American people, that I'm talking about. I'm talking about those
who, possessing money, fear risk and lose face because risk alone pays off in the end. I'm talking about
the world of money and immediate return, I'm talking about the gold curtain that is as hard as the iron
curtain, the gold curtain that separates America from
America, and America from Europe.

NEW YORK IS the best audience in the world. I have seen it, eager, attentive, laughing, enthusiastic, not quickly departing at the end but applauding the artists that pleased them. Nevertheless, the producer despises this audience. He declares them incapable of understanding high art and insists on making lowbrow work. If what he presents to the public seems too elevated, he cuts it, rearranges it, disrupts it, reduces it, defiles it into the form he imagines the audience wants, a public that doesn't even exist. Of course, the public is often deceived. They've been getting tricked now for a long time. They have excuses. No effort is made to educate them. But there are times when this instinctual public isn't deceived, and the producer pays dearly for his spite.

In Hollywood, after interminable discussions and despite his repugnance at composing music for a film, Stravinsky was about to come to terms with Mr. G——. Mr. G—— declared that he must also pay the arranger. "What arranger?" asked Stravinsky. Mr. G—— replied: "The one who will arrange your music."

This custom of arranging everything is your modus operandi. Above all, a work should not remain what it is. Hollywood is the origin of this phenomenon, which justifies itself by the pale blood of an aristocracy of filmmakers (technicians and artists) whose kingdom can no longer communicate with the outside world and whose race is exhausting itself.

This aristocracy, whose blood is becoming very pallid, exiles all minds too mysteriously crowned. Greta Garbo, Charlie Chaplin were the remarkable victims of this imperialist hive.

AMERICANS,

Human dignity is at stake. Be what you are. A people who preserved their childhood. A people young and honest. A people in whom the lifeblood circulates. Disentangle yourselves. Question others less and question yourselves more. Confide in your friends. Don't content yourself with those encounters where drinks are served but nothing is said. Don't disorient yourselves with vain activities. Don't surrender yourself to the lethal vertigo of radio and television. Television encourages the mind to stop chewing, to gulp down soft, predigested food. But the mind has robust teeth. Chew things with its robust teeth. Don't let them only serve as the ornamental smiles of the stars.

I VERY WELL know that you will reply: "Why don't you mind your own business, man of old Europe?" Of course I know that it's ridiculous to preach when what I deserve is for others to preach to me. I know Europe's faults better than I know yours. But there still exists in us a disorder that makes possible creation and surprise, a dunghill where our rooster braces its feet and which you mustn't confuse with a garbage heap, that fatal error our own government almost always proves guilty of making.

I DON'T FAIL to notice that we live in a barnyard and that you live in a bathroom. But, tell me, isn't it pleasant to one who lives in a barnyard to go into the bathroom, to one who lives in a bathroom to visit a barnyard? There's a common ground for our exchange. That's what I dream of, me, a man of the old French barnyard, me, the artisan who fabricates his object with his hands and carries it in his arms, in your city.

And, tell me, isn't it necessary for you to generalize a little and teach us your specialists' recipes? Isn't it necessary to entrust some of your machines to us, to see if we could humanize them, and to humanize yourselves by diminishing the prerogatives of your machines—in short, to tame our individualism and to arouse yours, so as to rise up together against false morals and bad habits, hand in hand?

Richard Wright spoke to the French people a few days ago and the things that he said weren't pleasant for anyone to hear. I know this trumpet from the Bible, this trumpet dear to the black people. When Louis Armstrong blows it, it swells to the cry of an angel. What is the meaning of this cry? What I'm trying to tell you. What comes of my visit to New York. A cry of anguish and love.

And maybe there is in my words something like an egotistical fear and a sort of instinct for preservation.

For the fate of the French is bound to your fate, and if the values that threaten you triumph, we are lost with you.

Neither priests nor New York psychiatrists are enough for us to unburden our conscience. The ones who go to confession, sin, and return to confession, just like the ones who empty themselves in the psychiatrist's office, reassure themselves of being empty, encumber themselves again with complexes, and go to empty themselves anew—both types foist themselves onto a world that excludes them.

Neither confession nor psychoanalysis should be envisioned as a comfort. It's an insult to the priests and the psychiatrists, and it wastes their time. I pity the innumerable people who undergo treatment for treatment's sake and refuse to get well.

I don't believe very much in your statistics. Did any one of you, the day before, expect to see President Truman reelected? And aren't the detectives of the Kinsey Report the psychiatrists of the impoverished, in whose presence you can actually see yourself, *boast* about yourself, invent yourself, make up a liberated version of yourself, adorned with imaginary vices, just as when a crime is committed in New York, in Chicago, in San Francisco, and thousands of people accuse themselves of it?

AMERICANS,

Admit that superfluity lightens the soul. Luxury is a noble virtue that you mustn't confuse with comfort. You have comfort. But you lack luxury. And don't say to me that currency plays a part. The luxury I encourage doesn't have anything to do with money. It can't be bought. It's the reward for those who don't dread discomfort. It's a commitment we make to our own selves. It's a pasture for the soul. It allows a young adult to wake up at dawn in a profound malaise, but without a shadow of bitterness or disgust.

AMERICANS,

I must now express to you my gratitude. New York welcomed me as more than a guest—it welcomed me as a friend.* From the minute I set foot in the city, I felt such a lightness of air where the skyscrapers hang their tulle and erect their hives flowing with golden honey. I repeat, everything is wide open in New York. Don't tell me it's because New York hasn't suffered (it's just a polite thing to say). Suffering never embellished anybody. The French aren't embellished—it's only because our wound is ugly that it will heal. No. Your good graces gush from an underground spring. Never, in my contacts with the most diverse milieus, did I hear neighbors slandered. Malicious gossip doesn't exist in New York, or if it does, it's not on display.

* I had, in Paris, received a telegram from Paul H. Buck asking me to be a professor, in French, at Harvard University, from 1949 to 1950.

THE DAY, THE sky of New York is coastal. The wind, the snow, the sun, the blue sky alternate at full speed. You're overwhelmed by the cold or the heat. At night, Broadway resembles a woman covered with jewels and agitated with nervous tics. Your streets are clogged with yellow taxis in electric tiaras that follow each other, assembling into a slow procession, incensed by mysterious vapors that elude the sun. The other night, I was contemplating your nocturnal city while driving inch by inch to the cinema where I was to introduce my film, *The Eagle with Two Heads.* I was hoping the obstacles on the road would pile up. You had reasons to avoid me. The play, adapted in England, transformed in America, staged quickly and badly, and cut by artists trying to save the staging without understanding you only lengthen what you cut, was a flop in New York.*

My English is too poor to express the difficult

---

* At the same time that your journalists, in regards to *The Eagle with Two Heads* (the play), were accusing me of lacking realism, the New York police were searching out two missing brothers. They found them, dead, barricaded in their house, where only the night could penetrate, by trapdoors and slides. One of them was dead from old age. The other was the victim of one of their traps. They had cluttered together the furniture, floor by floor, and automobiles were placed on top of one another, among trash cans, hats, and thousands of miscellaneous objects.

nuances required by my craft. So I had to mount the stage and speak in French. I invited Jean-Pierre Aumont to do me the kindness of appearing beside me and translating for me. From the first moment, I no longer felt the slightest shadow of embarrassment. The room moved and transported me. They curiously intuited my meanings, responding with applause and rendering the translator useless. Sometimes I asked Jean-Pierre to translate. He responded: "It's not worth it." The room laughed. An American cried: "Yes, yes, translate!" and a Frenchman translated from his seat. The atmosphere was what one wishes to have all the time in France, where the elite audience stays on guard and fears they're being mocked.

IF NEW YORK accepts you, it adopts you. I have never met such kindness (in the true sense of the word), such care, people who get on all fours to be helpful, sudden friendships, attentive curiosity, tender respect. Gifts and flowers filled my bedroom. I never had to pay anywhere, and if I insisted, the maîtres d'hôtel tore up my bills and refused to let me.

My film wasn't as successful as *Beauty and the Beast*. The *New York Times* film critic protested that he didn't understand it and demanded that I explain myself, but a number of letters arrived at the paper declaring that it was the critic's job to try to understand and that it was unacceptable to treat a guest so flippantly. In New York, the newspapers publish these sorts of letters and don't fear putting their chief critic in an awkward position.

I quickly saw where the misunderstanding was coming from about *The Eagle*. I've already said that New York loves labels. Mine's singular. *The Blood of the Poet* has been showing in New York for ten years. In *Beauty and the Beast*, the American public rediscovered the singularity of my old film in a more accessible form. So it's not surprising that it pleased them. *The Eagle* being a story that I invented and narrate myself, the American critics searched for a hidden meaning that couldn't be found, and, as a result, the film proved more disconcerting than an enigma. It became an insipid enigma.

I received at the hotel numerous exegeses of *The Blood of the Poet*. This film, shot twenty-nine years ago, became a classic among American filmmakers. They analyzed it, psychoanalyzed it, auscultated it, pored over its every seam. They don't understand the film, but it attracts them like a planchette tempts the interrogating hands of spiritualists. The study that Professor Werner Wolff devoted to it seemed the most brilliant; even though he committed a basic error, it was an error that didn't compromise the details. In effect, the professor, drawing on my book, *Opium*, claimed that opium's indirect associations composed the fabric of the film. Yet, this rhythm is natural for me—in a way it's the gait, the *swagger* of my spirit, and if opium, which I took at the prescribed amount without the least hint of intoxication, could have facilitated the associations and dissociations of ideas to which I abandon body and soul as soon as I decide on a project, it's in no way responsible for the system to which I've remained faithful, even when it's not obvious, over the long years when I haven't used drugs.

Whenever anyone talks to me about *The Blood of the Poet*, they use the term "surrealist." Maybe it's fashionable, but it's false. At that time, surrealism didn't exist, or, better, it has always existed but wasn't named yet.

Buñuel's film *The Age of Gold*, which opened at the same time as *The Blood of the Poet*, was shot from one angle while I shot mine from the other side. We only saw our respective films after their completion. And I didn't know of *The Andalusian Dog*, shot before *The Age of Gold*, until later. It would therefore be a mistake to search for Buñuel's influence on my film. It's important to understand that analogous waves are picked up by certain minds of the same period: these waves explain why works of art that stand opposed ferociously enough to the times, sometimes, in hindsight, appear related.

American critics have a hard time imagining that there can be within us a profound marriage of the conscious and the unconscious. On the contrary, Professor Wolff, author of a book on the unconscious and a book on the Easter Island, moves with a surprising agility in this world that is our own, that arises neither from sleep nor from waking, and that's populated with adorably ambiguous monsters. Never does he look for symbols—these symbols that reassure the public, permitting them to find an explanation for projects that are special precisely because they don't possess any symbolic meaning. Never does he try to decipher some rebus of sexuality. He even remarks, contrary to other translators of my visual language, that the film can't be analyzed from that angle, since the characters are *unsexed, glacial, and metaphysical*.*

As for the rest, can I reproach those who don't understand a film that I understand so poorly myself, and for misunderstanding it in 1949 when the American theaters have cut my film to simplify their program—and undoubtedly because they believe the film doesn't mean anything and that abridging it into a "digest" doesn't change anything? Yet, if the film remains an enigma to me, that makes it no different from most of our acts. But our acts are linked one to another by a red thread that we can't loosen or cut. And now young women from universities reproach me for not making similar films, and I need to explain to them, first, that the industrialization of filmmaking and the cost of films prevent youth and myself from using this confessional vehicle, and second, that my film, considered ridiculous at first, has since become a bible, so that redoing it would involve taking advantage of this stroke of luck rather than actually doing something new, and would upset those who liked the original precisely because that film tried to give the lie to an era when audacity visibly flaunted itself.

* Whereas in France one doesn't get hung up on the sexuality of film.

Is it my fault, people of New York and Paris, if you don't have my agile mind, if you treat me like an acrobat, because for forty years I've trained myself so that my soul is as fit and agile as the bodies of acrobats? And I congratulate myself that you are more familiar with my name than with my works, because knowledge of my works would lead you down the path of sleepwalkers, giving you vertigo, for which you'd never forgive me.

AMERICANS,

You're within a hair's breadth of understanding what Europe no longer understands. Everything predisposes you—my visit to New York proves to me that you're ceaselessly pacing back and forth in front of this rice-paper partition. So little is necessary for the miracle to occur, for your hunger for enigmas to lead you to punch a hole through this thin and subtle wall!

Then, you'd no longer question and would say to yourselves: "So that's how it was!" and you'd laugh—and your laughter would astonish the old world and the atomic bomb would seem childish next to this childish laughter.

As Nietzsche put it: *The ideas that change the face of the world come on the feet of doves.* A bomb, as atrocious as it may be, is a small affair compared to the insidious bombs that explode in our hearts. Take the example of Asian peoples who are oppressed because they refuse to make a deal with the devil, dizzy with the vertigo of numbers that mislead; since two and two do not make four—without arguing like poets that two and two make five—I'll leave to the meditation of businessmen how two and two can make twenty-two, emblem of Rothschild.

AMERICANS,

You graze the real world. Your sects, your clandestine religions, your phantoms, your fevers, your anguish, your disquiet, your crimes, and even your dread of Harlem's beautiful dances, reveal your desire. And yet you are ashamed of it. You hide it. So you sniff out your desire in blurry spectacles that nourish you in secret.

I saw you, Americans, leaving your seats at the end of Tennessee Williams's *A Streetcar Named Desire*, ashamed and fulfilled. I observed you out of the corner of my eye, seeing your women and your girls falling over backwards into the arms of the extraordinary actor Marlon Brando. I saw you searching for your nourishment in front of the magnificent mortal sins of Picasso. I saw you, Americans, letting your masks fall and straightening them with machines, as one plays a record on a jukebox in your popular bars. One day, if you accept this automatism, you will order food in one of these bars, you will pay for it, another will eat it for you, and you will be nourished without having chewed the meat. This will be the end of your world—the end of ours—the end of the world that the centuries have tethered to nothingness.

AMERICANS,

Your role is to save the old world that is so tough, so tender, that loves you and that you love. You role is to save the dignity of humanity. Your role is to fight and not to concede. Your role is to use your immense forces to aid the few heroes who are bleeding the white blood of the soul and the red blood that freezes in your veins. Your role is to vanquish the living dead who are descending the steps of the world with the cold indifference of this toy, this spring with which you amuse yourself by sending it tumbling down the staircases of your homes.

For such a task you'll need to shake yourselves out of it, to wake yourselves up, to become conscious. You can no longer consider art as a distraction, but instead as a priesthood. You must convince yourself that the artist finds first and seeks after. If you reach this stage, if you throw off *the yoke of being too free*, you'll escape ennui and laugh at its sad face. You'll tell yourself: "So it was just this sad face that frightened me, that encumbered me and filled me with emptiness." And you'll name it, and because you name it, it'll lose its hold over you.

And you'll make holes in the wall that separates you from enigmas, and since you'll inhabit the enigmas, they'll become familiar to you and you'll no longer fear them: you'll no longer court them and you'll possess them at ease, without needing to interrogate the sphinx.

AMERICANS,

It's my love that addresses these lines to you. It's my gratitude for your welcome that should serve as a warning not to read these words absentmindedly, not to confound them with a newspaper article or the work of an aesthete. Not to read my words while your radio runs a musical program titled: "Listen while you read."

The plane is passing through the auroras borealis. The hostess points it out to us. But I don't turn away from these lines that I trace, for, in my opinion, the aurora borealis of my dreams is more important than the aurora borealis of the sky.

AMERICANS,

Listen to the few men of Europe for whom words have the force of action. Don't reproach my insolence. I direct this insolence against myself above all, and I seek no excuses for the mistakes that I committed and that I'll never commit again.

The only thing I brag about is not being distracted, devouring what I see and retaining the details. It's the sin propagated by the modern press—they believe in the efficacy of lies, just as idiots believe intelligence requires maliciousness, that generosity is the synonym of stupidity, when the truth is that the surprising generosity of intelligence will always prevail over the conventional intelligence of malice.

That's the only point where I could permit myself to give you counsel. The only point over which my experience is wide and long. The only point where malice won't affect me, since it gets everything wrong about me, trying to torment me with a false effigy that can't cause me the least evil.

Be attentive, Americans. I have in mind a type of attention less academic than yours. Be attentive to the profound lineage of beings, more than to their endeavors, which only reveal fragments. Our acts are valuable only for their continuity, for the prior stages that cause them. It's quite natural that some rare manifestations of Europe reach you, encouraging you to take us for weather vanes. It's the fault of poorly organized exchanges, maladroit translations, barren plains that stretch out before your eyes from one work to another, that appear to you without any links between them, like the wreckage of a ship. The fact that you attach some price to this flotsam should make it plain why we are grateful and astonished when you manage to recognize the basic form of a maritime accessory.

I'm not demanding your attention, but some assistance, so that the comings and goings among our peoples become more fluid. Instead of your attention, I ask you to bring to the attention of your leaders the importance of organizing an unencumbered route where culture won't be halted at Customs and the Exchange Office.

FRANCE IS INTERESTED exclusively in your books, in passionately reading the writers who you hardly esteem; and I know of New Yorkers who are ignorant of recent American fashion trends that are already part of our customs. Pay us back in kind. Don't let the obstacles multiply, and don't be content to get a sense of France through a brief visit like mine. Your book sales are in crisis. So be it. And ours? Nevertheless your books and your poets circulate in France, translated everywhere.

It's gotten to the point that our real literature is like chamber music, a secret music best passed from hand to hand, under the table. Your endeavors of the same order have all the trouble in the world taking shape: America sooner finds billions to sponsor a huge catastrophe than the little it would cost for an authentic creation. It's true that beauty remains cursed in all its forms, insinuating itself fraudulently—what ends up lasting never comes into the world with the ease of what won't. But you're the people that consecrate the hazardous ventures of Europe. Your power is without bounds. My ultimate prayer will be then to ask you to be attentive to the new that hasn't proven itself, and, since you hang from the walls of your museums the marvelous nonsense of our youth, to also permit our more recent marvelous nonsense to slip into America on the feet of the doves that Nietzsche preferred over the racket of platoons and their weapons.

AMERICANS,

I saw the first films. I heard the first phonographs. I created, with Roland Garros, the first aerial acrobatics. Ever since—except for what concerns the atom—progress has replaced invention. Everything changes. A world is going to end. A world begins. It's in your hands to decide if it will be one of darkness or light. There isn't a minute to lose.

What is the nightmare of your city that sleeps standing up, I ask you? The atomic bomb. It exists and you don't want it to exist. You don't talk about it at your dinner table any more than you'd talk about rope at the home of the hanged. And since you need to apologize for its existence, you descend unconsciously this modern slope towards the death of thought.* Because

* It's the reason for the success of ballets in New York where gesticulation seeks to replace words.

49

if thought were dead, the explosives would only destroy emptiness—they would no longer kill anything.

I don't admire a race unto itself. A race is neither bad nor good. I like a race only if it's oppressed. For, even if innumerable, if it's oppressed, a race represents a minority. A minority will always prevail in my heart over a majority, since a majority always oppresses a minority as a result of some perceived superiority, and in reaction to the remorse provoked by this minority.

A race that oppresses another is detestable. If the oppressed race oppresses in turn, it too will become detestable. Don't you understand that we are eternally on the wrong side of the barricade, us other minorities of old Europe, and that this wrong side will prevail in the long run, in these times that disturb you, you who want to live in the present, in love with fame and success?

You won't be saved by guns or by fortune. You will be saved by the minority of those who think. By your secret souls, by your hidden treasures, by your madness that Edgar Allan Poe summed up, in short, by your poets—regardless of what ink they use—and your filmmakers aren't the least of your inks, an ink of light that false morals drench with water and prevent from flourishing.

Everywhere, in America, a minority palpitates and finds itself prisoner to a fake freedom.

It would take only a stroke of luck for your complexes, your Protestant reserve, your fears to disappear, for your spirit to burgeon, pullulate, explode *without control*, with the enormous eroticism of springtime in your countrysides of the South.

Don't forget, the rhythm of the world respires like your chest, its lungs dilate and contract in turn. We are victims of an era of emptying lungs. The world *expires*. It doesn't think anymore; it *spends*. Its breath destroys its harvest. Wait until it fills its lungs anew.

Your national questionnaire begins, if I don't mistake myself: "What do you think of the American woman?" Not that a brief sojourn in New York authorizes me to reply. But, if this question opens the questionnaire, it's without doubt because women occupy a high place in America—your regiment of men is kept in line by a female drum major.

In France, men grow without transition from schoolboys into old men. In America a bitter struggle obliges men to live, from childhood until death, in middle age, the age of separation from the mother. Man rediscovers in marriage a mother before whom he bows his head.

When a New York couple invites us over, when the elevator brings us to the antechamber, the mistress of the house comes to meet us. A bit hunched, a tad anonymous, the husband hides behind her.

In France, before 1900, a woman submitted to

54

the exigencies of cooking and procreating. She got
bent out of shape with use. She was a utensil and not
yet an object of art. 1900 marks the triumph of the
woman. The Parisian woman dominates the monu-
mental door of the Exposition. In the Grand Palais
and in the Petit Palais, nude women, of stone and
bronze, straddle steeds, led by men reduced to the
state of grooms holding the reins. Impressionism will
be the highest glory of the feminine style.

When the Fauves and the Cubists restored the
stronger sex to its former place, with their cruel
knights multicolored and armored with newspapers, the weak sex, determined to not give an inch,
changed into a boy, cutting her hair and giving herself over to strenuous sports.

New York offers the spectacle of a medley of
feminine art objects, women upon whom men attach their fortunes, feminine idols, covered with the
spoils of the vanquished enemy, and sportive girls,
such as I admired, acting in a play that unfolds in a
college where, more terrible than the worst of the
boys, they charm us with their waists, their skirts,
and their superb walk in the manner of bohemians
who read palms.

And since your censorship rests upon the tribunals
of women, I'm forced to revise my verdict and sup-
pose that censorship must be agreeable to you, since

every impediment levels out your slope of luxury, obliging you to overcome obstacles: the impossibility for you to say certain things pushes you to invent other things to say, like in the films of Sturges, where he slips mischievously between your judges with a dancer's insolent grace. It must not be forgotten that work loves constraints and that the censorship of the Church gave rise, among the painters of Renaissance Italy, to secrets and rebuses thousands of times more suggestive than if they'd been expressed without detour.

CHARLES BAUDELAIRE, WHO gave us your Edgar Allan Poe, speaks, in the preface that introduces his translation, of decadence as proof of an extreme civilization. Me, old European, decadent and proud to be, at the risk of appearing pessimistic to you (the pessimist is one, in your world, to whom you give the finger, one blacklisted), at the risk, I say, of making myself guilty of the crime of pessimism—which comes over me with the force of optimism and out of fear that things appear better than they are—I advise you to read this preface.

I quote a paragraph of it:

. . . .

But what the certified professors haven't realized is that, in the movement of life, some complication, some combination can present itself, all of a sudden, unforeseen by their schoolboy wisdom. And so their insufficient language is found defective, as in the case—a phenomenon that will perhaps increase in variety—in which a nation begins with decadence, starting where the others finish.

Since between the immense colonies of the present century new literatures are developing, there will most certainly arise spiritual accidents of a nature disturbing to the academic mind. Young and old at the same time, America gossips and prattles with a surprising volubility. Who could count her poets?

They're innumerable. Her bluestockings? They clut-
ter the reviews. Her critics? Trust that she has ped-
ants as valuable as ours for ceaselessly reminding
the artist of ancient beauty, for questioning a poet
or a novelist about the morality of their purpose and
the merit of their intentions. There as here, but even
more than here, literati don't know how to spell; a
puerile activity, pointless; compilers of cornucopia,
hack writers, plagiarists of plagiaries and critics of
critiques. Amidst this maelstrom of mediocrities, in
this world enamored with material perfections—the
scandal of a new genre that makes legible the gran-
deur of lazy people—amidst this society eager for
surprises, in love with life, but above all with a life full
of excitement, a man appeared who was great, not
only because of his metaphysical subtlety, the sinister
or ravishing beauty of his conceptions, or the rigor of
his analysis, but great also and no less great at cari-
cature. I should explain myself with some care; for
recently an imprudent critic made use, to disparage
Edgar Allan Poe and to undermine the sincerity of
my admiration, of the word "juggler" which I myself
had applied to the noble poet as a eulogy.

. . . .

This sensational preamble could serve as our de-
fense against those who treat us like decadents. It will
light your lantern. You will see, under the flickering

light of the man responsible for it, what's at stake in this eternal confusion between the juggler and the thinker, between an agile thought and the gesture of an illusionist.

If you listen with an attentive ear—and I don't doubt you do—you will discover the reason why, no matter whether it's Picasso, Paul Éluard, André Breton, Aragon, Sartre, Jean Genet or myself (I cite on purpose men whose activities are in opposition to one another), the singular attitude of artists and the unique point of view from which they express themselves is all too hastily interpreted by the frivolous as a magical process for avoiding the anguish of work. In short, the attitude of nonchalance that crowns all genuine labor tricks the whole world into believing it's as easy to create as it appears.

The more you're blessed, the more you'll overcome yourself, the more you'll fight against the gift that predisposes your ink to run too quickly, the more you'll strive to harness and contain it.

FRANCE IS PERPETUALLY in a fight with herself. This is what shocks me. The great French tradition is one of anarchy. It's the sturdiest tradition. Disorder permits France to live in the same way that order is indispensable for other peoples. I am amused by people who fear France is becoming a village. She always was. She always will be. She already was under Louis XIV.

A village with its café of Commerce, its newspaper kiosk and its tobacco shop where everyone discusses and disputes.

It's from this perpetual conflict that a fire is born with the mild, intense light which Guillaume Apollinaire said the eye could tirelessly scrutinize all the way to the bottom.

From the outside it causes consternation and gives the impression of a confused haze. The stranger sees only groups that oppose each other, personalities that contradict each other, individuals that insult each other. But doesn't anyone realize how it's like boiling water, whose bubbles arise with an iridescence that can't be found anywhere else?

In France, everyone thinks. Even stupidity thinks. All the world takes the stage. Few people are in the audience—it's rare that our public doesn't declare it can do better than us. But this surprising lack of discipline does offer advantages. France actually is one of the only countries where the crowd might grant a play success simply because journalists condemn it. Nobody believes anybody and I dare say that the spirit of contradiction, carried to this extreme, drives the crowd to take the contrarian view and applaud over the jeering.

I HAVE OFTEN written that the spirit of creation is none other than the spirit of contradiction in its highest form. In effect, a great work opposes the preceding work and contradicts it—and this doesn't prevent the preceding work from living, breathing, taking root, and blooming in its time, too. And so on and so forth. It's necessary to remember this Hebrew proverb: "Equilibrium engenders inertia. It's out of disequilibrium that changes are born."

That's the secret of the most celebrated architecture. Of Versailles, of Venice, of Amsterdam. The plumb line killed the humanity of facades with their charming and asymmetrical resemblances to faces. Each one *expressed* itself and wobbled divinely.

There's a great danger in desiring order and in not adopting a manner of disorder through which the soul can disentangle itself, rather than drying out on deadlines.

In the country I came across an old copy of the Goncourt *Journals*. I opened it and found this note: "A friend arrives from New York and announces to us a piece of news that we don't dare believe and that would be the end of everything. *The sinks stick to the walls.*" Nowadays, such a remark provokes laughter. Then we dream about the same thing and begin to fear such developments may be the source of some of our misfortunes.

Humankind must obey the order to use the washroom, like the ox to the stable, the horse to the hayrack. Our will yields and cripples us. Once upon a time, water, light, and food were brought to us; we didn't have to change places. We were left to our couch and our book. Manual labor was gracious and infinite. There was something for everyone. But manual labor disappeared. The machine supplanted it. The faucet killed the water-carrier. And thus tragedy. If the faucet works well in America, it works very badly in France.

Our weakness, then, will be to envy and imitate the nations of discipline and order. Our strength will be to admit our disorder and our lack of discipline, to draw resources from both.

Since the work of the filmmaker is in my eyes a form of manual labor, each second bearing on the smallest detail, it would be impossible for me to express myself in a country of order, that is to say of specialized labor, divided into boxes and restricted to one place or another by union rules. I would clear the set or I would oblige my team to go on strike. This is what counsels me to refuse the bidding of Hollywood where trade-unionism exerts itself so rigorously.

Here, in France, the disorder of which I speak permits me to touch everything in a film and slip past any obstacles. If something is in the realm of the impossible because of our old equipment, I hand it over to my workers. Even if it's the least among them who tries to make possible the impossible, they almost always succeed, thanks to natural resourcefulness and ingenuity—most often it's an electrician who aids the machinist or a machinist who aids the electrician. With Christian Bérard I would sometimes choose my extras among the machinists, to obtain from their good graces a special favor unimaginable in a nation subjected to strict regulations.

Alas, it's normal when an ingenious country is stifled in any way, imposed upon to the point of absurdity, hollowed out with pitfalls by taxes and the police, that ingenuity expends itself under the form of fraudulence until crooks become poets in a way. You can't imagine how much genius is wasted by the day in France to dupe everybody and to profit by methods analogous to those of poets wielding numbers. I'd guess that poets were the first victims of swindlers' mysterious lyricism. It's often the case that I get duped, only to feel admiration for my thief and tell myself that it's necessary to find for my work, which consists of giving, resources as nimble as those of work that consists of taking.

Not that I extol crooks; but I note that, even when

France teeters toward the edge, she still leans with a certain genius and finds a way to put into motion, against the grain, a suitably old mechanism that never ceases to surprise the world.

Our universe evolves in crests and troughs. If there's a crest, there will be a trough. It's a matter of patience—I don't think that an injured country, with a wound that's mending, gets better in a couple of weeks. It's therefore absurd to pretend that France is declining. France, after what it has suffered, is a mending wound. It's the term a doctor uses to describe an injury that's healing. It doesn't mean the wound looks ugly and is developing gangrene. On the contrary, a wound that isn't mending is a dangerous wound, one that only gives the appearance of health. It misleads people who tend to be reassured by their own immobility and who have never observed the terrible workings of plants, sap, and bark.

Sergei Diaghilev led the multicolored and famous troupe of the Ballets Russes across the world. He declared to me: you've never really put on a spectacle if you haven't done it in Paris. It is, he said, the only capital where the shows can provoke lovers' quarrels.

I know well that in 1949 politics plays a considerable role and that the bickering of parties outweighs lovers' quarrels, but between you and me, don't these disputes seem just as unfair and in bad faith as lovers' quarrels? It's still a good disorder, a good cleavage, a good tempest, a rich manure, a fertilizer that makes the plants burst, to the left, to the right, below, above, spreading their seeds no matter where. And it's this "no matter where" that counts.

Propaganda exploits this method, but it's a conscious exploitation—only when done unconsciously can such dispersals of seeds succeed in the long run.

It would be funny to cite for you, among others, the names of poets who honor France and ensure her true prestige. They're men that she hounds with her police or her disdain: Racine, Villon, Baudelaire, Rimbaud, Ducasse, Nerval, Verlaine ... the game is too easy. So many downfalls, hospitalizations, desperate retreats to cloisters, departures, suicides, catastrophes.

If things had changed, there would've been discipline, order, fear, comfort ... all qualities that France, I repeat, doesn't possess and that would cause its ruin. France is bristling with valleys and peaks. You can't imagine a flat France. Besides, if anyone attempted to flatten her, they'd never succeed. If you try, she bristles. It's fortunate there are those who desire to flatten her. Because a country that records and reveres its disorder becomes a country of the dead. Its accidents assume the role of principles and its people resemble plants reading treatises on horticulture.

France would have everything to lose by pursuing resources unsuitable to it—for example, by claiming to have a major industry. Its prerogatives are artisanship, invention, discovery, accident. Accident especially, son of disorder, which breaks the straight line and leads to surprises, giving unpredictable meanings to things, things that the French continue naively to call miracles.

AMERICANS,

In France, a certain fixation on disparaging ourselves is still one of our secret weapons. If France didn't scorn her products, she would be the vainest and most intolerable nation. But she imitates florists who don't keep flowers in their houses, perfumers who dread perfume, seamstresses who don't wear their own dresses. This earns her an air of reserve and would enable her products to flourish elsewhere if the Exchange Office didn't object to our rhythm.

France, for many centuries, believed herself beloved. She wasn't at all. Now that she's loved, she still thinks she's despised.

And of course some of her products, which she disdains, perpetuate her profound glory. There are countless seeds that she lets fall from her bag, which get blown away and serve her without her knowledge.

Exchanges between countries, as soon as they no longer rely on a financial system, are almost impossible, and the cinema remains perhaps the only domain where visual syntax (its genuine syntax) establishes a sort of terror.

It's then that the waves are set in motion, wavelengths that few radio stations pick up—they resist the official control of success or failure, and their influence is without measure or limit. One would be quite wrong not to be on guard against them, not to distrust them, for they insinuate themselves silently into the tumult of the day. Who tunes in to these waves? The few ears that listen to everything that the rest don't hear at all. It's these ears that count; authentic French mouths speak only for these ears. This must be what Nietzsche called our chamber music. This must be what makes it common to say, in every age of our History, that art is dead and that nothing more is happening.

This nose squashed by the prospects—this lack of hindsight saves each era, since art wouldn't know how to bloom in the sun, but mysteriously manages to grow secretly in the shadows, even if its creator is dangerously in public view. In such a case, the name of the author masks their writings and wards off the pests.

The study of these mechanisms of art should fascinate the critics. They could become art's chemists and naturalists instead of its chroniclers.

THAT SAID, I add, since Frenchmen never resigns themselves to parting with their interlocutors, following one false farewell with another, in a Mediterranean manner, as they linger on the stairs—I add, I say, that I've acquired the certainty (a certainty that's suited to me and that I don't ask anybody to share) that the planet I inhabit belongs to a system, that the system is solid, that every solid is made of the same stuff as stars, and that its molecules are separated by the same spaces and the same ether that our small-mindedness makes us believe is unfathomable. And this astronomical system to which our world belongs is but the material of some part, some object, some world superior to ours, a world that finds itself likewise in a very modest position in comparison to other systems, and so on without end. In short, that God thinks us and doesn't think about us. For honesty's sake, I must confess to you my reservations about discussing these problems of the terrestrial order, parochial in some way and without the slightest importance except insofar as the duty of humankind is to live on our own scale and to busy ourselves with our own concerns (which still comes down to a matter of what we believe does not concern us). In the grand scheme of things, even the most appalling atomic bomb must be only some firecracker on the hide of a rhinoceros, horrible only on our small scale:

even admitting that such an explosive could unravel our celestial system, it wouldn't unravel anything all that significant—it would merely form rust on the surface of the object that contains us.

And therefore, since the game played by humankind is only as important as we imagine, it's difficult for me to take seriously the preoccupation of dictators or any person mad for glory. The reflections that I have just made on France, the order, the disorder, the old world, the new world, the theater and the cinema, must be understood, from Michelangelo to the mechanical rabbit, as an homage to the vertiginous skill exerted by my peers to distract themselves on the train that carries us all toward death.

THE EARTH MUST be a great deal younger than is generally thought—those that love to destroy or construct still have plenty of time to invent verses and catastrophes.

The earth seems old to us. She must be sixteen years old in comparison to the duration of a human life. She's at the age of schoolyard scuffles; all fun and games, until someone gets hurt. Without doubt she was, in the time of ancient Egypt, at the age of sandcastles by the seaside. In the days of the Greek philosophers, she was at the age of questioning her parents. Our good fortune is to be spared from living on earth when she reaches the age of reason. It's the dreariest age of all.

I very well know that it's tiresome to live in dangerous times. I'm not so naive as to think the time of wars is over, that people will manage to live hand in hand. And the fault doesn't lie with anyone. Responsibility for this order of things is just a way of reassuring yourself, of nourishing your pride. Humans fight each other by nature—they imitate animals, plants and microbes. But I dislike the tendency to fear that one war will follow another. Such fears are harmful to undertakings that can honor a world which war dishonors. It serves as an excuse for laziness, as people say to themselves: "What's the good of working and creating since destruction is coming?"

I salute your optimism. My pessimism is merely a form of optimism. I'd rather things happened otherwise, and there are times that I weep on the ruins. Afterwards I think the ruins have a great beauty that surprises and inspires us in some unexpected artistic direction. Cities of solid gold must sleep under the sands. The earliest ages may well be the last vestiges of advanced civilizations. Let's get used to humility in the face of such an incomprehensible system, and since we can't climb the ladder of angels, let us resign ourselves to our own ladder that we owe it to ourselves to climb to its highest echelons.

It's quite ridiculous, as well, to speak of decadence on a land which results from decadence. In fact, light results from decomposition. As soon as a star ceases to be in a nebulous state (grows old in some way), it decomposes and ignites. When the fire dies down and retreats inward, the star crusts over. In a state of decadence and decay, the land gives birth to life. The star swarms with vermin. That's us.

AMERICANS,

I write, I write, and the passengers sleep, curled up in the penumbra. I benefit by writing you from a no-man's-land, outside of any territory, in a nocturnal sky that still simulates some zone of liberty. I deliberately write in a conversational tone, as if my fellow passengers could hear me and respond. I write by repeating myself, by contradicting myself, by trying to work out faint ideas that don't flow well through these modern channels: of the politician or the philosopher. I avoid doctrine and without a doubt you'll just barely see what emerges from my words, since I have no desire to draw out their meanings—if something emerges, it'll do so all on its own.

Before the spectacle of universal governance our French liberties shrink. I believe, it seems to me, I've adequately explained what still protects us. But your example would be decisive if you acknowledged that your liberty means that you are also free to not be free, if you accepted that someone governs you and deprives you of liberty.

One of the last free men is speaking to you, free with all that it requires of solitude and loneliness. I can't pretend to be supported by any group, by any school, by any Church, by any party. My soapbox is in this ether that the plane ravages with its propellers, a platform surrounded by cruel stars and people who slumber and who, on solid ground, each have a milieu and an opinion. I possess neither opinion nor milieu. I address myself always to those who struggle desperately to be free and who must, like me, expect to be slapped on both cheeks, to the point of asking themselves, when they're complimented, if they aren't guilty of some error.

AMERICANS,

I'm going to try to sleep and to dream. I love to live my dreams and forget them upon waking. For there I inhabit a world where control doesn't yet exist. It will exist if you keep going down the same direction. Dreams will be controlled—and not by psychiatrists, but by the police. Dreams will be controlled and they will be punished. They will punish the act of dreaming.

Good night.

JEAN COCTEAU.
PARIS—NEW YORK
(AIR FRANCE)
JANUARY 12–13, 1949